Independent DAMES

WHAT YOU NEVER KNEW ABOUT THE WOMEN AND GIRLS OF THE AMERICAN REVOLUTION

by Laurie Halse Anderson

illustrated by Matt Faulkner

SIMON & SCHUSTER BOOKS FOR YOUNG READERS · NEW YORK LONDON TORONTO SYDNEY

SIMON & SCHUSTER BOOKS FOR YOUNG READERS
An imprint of Simon & Schuster Children's Publishing Division
1230 Avenue of the Americas, New York, New York 10020

Book design by Lucy Ruth Cummins
The text for this book is set in Caslon Antique.
The illustrations for this book are rendered in watercolor and pen and ink.
Manufactured in the United States of America
2 4 6 8 10 9 7 5 3 1
Library of Congress Cataloging-in-Publication Data
Anderson, Laurie Halse.
Independent dames : what you never knew about the women and girls of the American Revolution /
by Laurie Halse Anderson ; illustrated by Matt Faulkner.—1st ed.
p. cm.
ISBN-13: 978-0-689-85808-6 (hardcover)
ISBN-10: 0-689-85808-6 (hardcover)
1. United States—History—Revolution, 1775–1783—Women—Juvenile literature.
2. United States—History—Revolution, 1775–1783—Participation, Female—Juvenile literature. 3. United States—History—Revolution, 1775–
1783—Biography—Juvenile literature. 4. Women—United States—History—18th century—Juvenile literature.
5. Women—United States—Biography—Juvenile literature. 6. Girls—United
States—History—18th century—Juvenile literature. 7. Girls—United States—
Biography—Juvenile literature. I. Faulkner, Matt, ill. II.
Title.
E276.A53 2008
973.3'082—dc22
20070426

Acknowledgments
The publisher thanks Jim Heins and Peter Golia at the Oneida Nation for their insights.
For more information about the Oneida Nation, write to them at 223 Genesee Street, Oneida, New York 13241
or visit their website at www.oneidanation.net.

★ *Dedicated to my Revolutionary grandmothers* ★

Phoebe Wicks Carver—b. 1759 CT, m. 1/29/1777
Hannah Marsh Chamberlin—b. 11/9/1729 Sutton, MA, d. 1/1791 Royalston, MA
Desire Fisk Cole—b. 5/15/1735 Scituate, RI, m. 1/12/1755
Rebecca Remsey Fetterly—m. 10/26/1784 Schoharie, NY
Catherina Snethezinger Fredendall—b. 1754 Middleburg, NY
Abigail Rice Gale—b. 10/7/1746 Worcester, MA, d. 1786 VT
Esther Cunningham Gale—b. 6/18/1699 Watertown, MA, d. 7/16/1782 Weston, MA
Hannah Knowlton Holcomb—b. 9/18/1776 New Ipswich, NH, d. 10/1/1847 Lewis, NY
Mary Mercy Holcomb—b. 5/31/1740 Simsbury, CT, d. 10/30/1826 Granby, CT
Phoebe Wright Knowlton—b. 11/20/1728 Westford, MA, d. 1/1813 Ipswich, NH
Hannah Rockwell Lewis—b. 6/25/1755 Middleton, CT, d. 2/7/1803 Elizabethtown, NY
Elizabeth Cole Mason—b. 11/10/1759 Scituate, RI, d. 9/17/1838 Ft. Ann, NY
Elizabeth Wood Mason—b. 1729 Rehobeth, MA, d. 3/22/1812
Elizabeth Flagg Rice—b. 5/24/1717 Waltham, MA, d. 8/3/1792 Worcester, MA
Eunice Knowlton Rice—b. 1/28/1769 New Ipswich, NH, d. Lewis, NY
Susanna Allen Rice—b. 1/22/1732 Sudbury, MA, d. 12/17/1823 Ashburnham, MA
Abigail Chamberlin Stockwell—b. 6/28/1765 Sutton, MA, d. 2/27/1853 Hartford, NY
Rachel Kenney Stockwell—b. 12/23/1737 Sutton, MA, d. 1812, MA
Ruth Hammond Tobey—b. 4/14/1765 Rochester, MA
Dinah Hart Woodruff—b. 11/9/1738 Northington, CT
Sally Healy Russell Woodruff—b. 1/18/1780 VT, d. 12/15/1850 Lewis, NY
Sarah Woodford Woodruff—b. 6/4/1714 Farmington, CT, d. 11/28/1790 Farmington, CT
—L. H. A.

*Dedicated to the memory of my Uncle Lewis Powers—
decorated World War II marine fighter pilot*
—M. F.

Look, another school play about the heroes of the American Revolution. How sweet.

We've got George Washington, Thomas Jefferson, John Adams, Ben Franklin, and Thomas Paine. Famous guys who did important things.

Wonderful. Just wonderful.

Of course, you're missing part of the story.

In fact, you're missing about half of it.

4

Who's Who

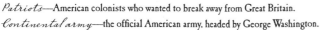

Patriots—American colonists who wanted to break away from Great Britain.

Continental army—the official American army, headed by George Washington.

Militia—independent regional groups of men who fought with the Continental army but were not under Washington's command. The people of the Oneida Nation also fought with American militia and Continental army troops.

Continental Congress—representatives of the rebel Thirteen Colonies who made up the new government until almost the end of the war.

Parliament—elected legislature of Great Britain.

British army—Troops under British command, made up of British and German (Hessian) soldiers, as well as Loyalist Americans, who did not want independence, and some Native American tribes.

Loyalists—Historians now believe that about 20 percent of Americans did not want to form an independent country. They were the Loyalists, who helped the British. They were also called *Tories*.

1763
· French and Indian War ends, leaving the British government in desperate need of cash.
· Proclamation of 1763 prohibits American colonists from settling west of the Appalachian Mountains. Americans are not happy about this.
· Charles Mason and Jeremiah Dixon begin surveying the Mason-Dixon Line between Pennsylvania and Maryland.

1764
· British Parliament passes the Sugar Act to raise money from American colonies.
· Parliament passes the Currency Act to prevent colonists from issuing their own money.
· At meetings in Massachusetts and Virginia, colonists complain about the unfairness of the Acts.

Hello? How about the women?
What about the girls?
They wanted a free country too. They worked, they argued, they fought, and they suffered—just like the men and the boys.

They didn't teach you this yet?

Listen up.

A couple of centuries ago, Great Britain bossed America around. Americans didn't like it. Not one bit.

1765
· Parliament passes the Stamp Act, taxing Americans directly for the first time.
· Parliament passes the Quartering Act, forcing Americans to give British soldiers a place to live and food.
· Boycotts and anger spread as violent mobs protest. "No taxation without representation" becomes a popular slogan.

1766
· Protests cause the British to repeal the hated Stamp Act.
· Americans celebrate the repeal of the Stamp Act with bell ringing and bonfires. Boycotts are relaxed. Everybody is calmer.
· Parliament passes the Declaratory Act, emphasizing that it has supreme authority to rule American colonies.

American men held meetings and wrote letters and sent politicians to ask the British to treat us fairly. Didn't work.

American women stopped buying British stuff. It was a boycott. (Maybe we should call it a girlcott. Or a ladycott.)

Buying British fabric became a big fashion "no." Making homemade cloth was the cool thing to do. Tea drinking slowed to a drip as patriotic families turned to chocolate, coffee, and cider. Tempers started to boil.

THE NERVE!

Women and girls calling themselves *Daughters of Liberty* gathered in homes and on town squares for spinning bees. The thread and yarn they spun were woven into homespun cloth, which rebel Americans wore with pride. *Mary Torr Thompson* and her neighbors spun, wove, and sewed enough clothing for a whole company of soldiers.

8

1769
· Virginia's House of Burgesses condemns British actions in Massachusetts. Declares that only Virginia's government can tax its citizens.
· Britain orders the House of Burgesses shut down.

1767
· Parliament passes the Townshend Acts, taxing glass, lead, paint, paper, and, most significantly, tea. The taxes paid for British military expenses in America.
· Americans begin another round of boycotting the British.
· Parliament dissolves the New York Assembly because it refused to support the Quartering Act.
· The survey of the Mason-Dixon line is completed. The line, extended in 1784, was later known as the dividing line between free and slave states.

1768
· Massachusetts Circular Letter calls for the colonies to join together and resist unfair taxation.
· More British troops arrive in Boston.
· John Dickinson publishes "The Liberty Song," which is sung at patriotic political gatherings and celebrations. The song includes the lines: "Then join hand in hand, brave Americans all! By uniting we stand, by dividing we fall."
· From a poem by *Hannah Griffitts*: "Let the Daughters of Liberty nobly arise."
· The word "boycott" was first used in the late 1800s. The colonists who refused to buy British goods in protest of new taxes call their actions "nonimportation" or "nonconsumption."

When nine-year-old *Susan Boudinot* and her mother were served tea at the mansion of the royal governor of New Jersey, Susan curtsied politely and pretended to sip. Then she threw the tea out the window.

- Most of the Townshend Acts are repealed, but tensions are still high.
- British soldiers and Americans riot on Golden Hill in New York City.
- British soldiers kill several Americans during the Boston Massacre, a protest that turned deadly.
- *Betsy Foote* and *Charity Clarke* both wrote that spinning and knitting made them feel "Nationly."
- More than three hundred Boston women signed an agreement not to use tea in their homes.

- British goods boycotted by the Americans included paper, glass, lead, paint, tea, wine, indigo, sugar, gloves, hats, fabric, shoes, coaches and carriages, rope, ship anchors, linseed oil, and glue.
- Boycotts and protests weren't always peaceful. Mobs of women and men broke into shops selling British imports, destroyed the goods, and chased the shopkeepers out of town. Women joined the mobs that tarred and feathered British sympathizers.

- One group of women "tarred and feathered" a young man who criticized the Continental Congress while they were working at a quilting bee. Instead of hot tar and feathers, the women used molasses and weeds. If a merchant tried to make an unfair profit by charging too much for staples like bread and coffee, a large group of women would storm his shop and threaten him until he changed his prices.

The British were mad. After lots of arguing and name-calling, war broke out—the American Revolution.

Everybody thought the British would win because the American Army was tiny and pathetic.

The first battles were disasters for the Americans. British soldiers marched into Boston, New York City, and Philadelphia. They took over houses, too; moved in without even asking.

American moms had to cook for them and wash their clothes. Sounds awful, doesn't it?

Phillis Wheatley was an African slave who became one of the most famous poets of the Revolution. In 1775 she sent George Washington a poem written in his honor, and she later met with him. Phillis's interaction with Washington might have helped influence his changing attitude about slavery.

10

1771
· British skirmish with rebellious Americans in North Carolina.
· Americans continue to protest British actions.

1772
· Committees of Correspondence form so colonies can communicate about ways to rebel against the British.
· Americans attack the *Gaspee*, a British ship that ran aground off Rhode Island.

- Parliament passes the Tea Act, forcing Americans to pay tea tax and prevent tea smuggling.
- To protest the Tea Act, a group of men dressed as Mohawk Indians dump 342 crates of tea into Boston Harbor.
- Daniel Boone leads settlers into Kentucky. The group is attacked by Native Americans frustrated by the invading pioneers.

Yankee Doodle's dear ol' mum, was spying on the Redcoats.

American agents spying on the British in Philadelphia smuggled notes to *"Mom" Rinker*, who buried the notes deep in balls of yarn. Mom liked to knit on a cliff, where she laid out her linen to bleach in the sun. While knitting, she would let her yarn with the secret notes roll off the cliff to the American soldiers waiting below.

No way—it was great!

When the soldiers talked about their battle plans, the moms secretly listened in. They hid coded messages about the plans in buttons, bags of flour, and balls of yarn. Then they snuck the messages to American officers.

Spy moms and daughters did more than eavesdrop. They stole official messages, counted weapons and troops, carried military instructions, watched for war ships, and spread the word when the British marched.

The spying moms and daughters ruined the best plans of the enemy. The British were furious! They offered cash rewards for captured spies. Passing secrets became deadly work. The British killed the spies they caught—male or female.

SPREAD OUT, LADS—
THE ICE IS THIN!

Elizabeth Burgin helped two hundred American prisoners of war escape from a deadly prison ship by leading the men across the frozen ice of New York Harbor in the middle of the night. The British were furious and put a price on her head. Elizabeth had to flee to avoid being hanged.

13

· Four months after the Boston Tea Party, residents of New York City dump eighteen chests of tea to protest the unfair British taxes.
· The Intolerable Acts punish Massachusetts colonists for their acts of protest.
· Other colonies send food and money to Massachusetts.
· More boycotts begin in response to the Intolerable Acts.

· First Continental Congress meets in Philadelphia to discuss a stronger response to British actions.
· Militias form in Massachusetts to fight the British.
· Washington's famous Culper spy ring had many women in it who would pass on messages hidden in baskets of food or shopping.
· Poet *Annis Boudinot Stockton* wrote "Tho' a female, I was born a patriot and cant help it If I would."

· Commenting on the changes that the war made to the lives of women, *Eliza Wilkinson* wrote "none were greater politicians than the several knots of ladies, who met together. All trifling discourse of fashions, and such low chat was thrown by, and we commenced perfect statesmen."

Women and girls were the support troops behind the American Army. They made sure the men had food, clothes, and shoes. They melted down knives, forks, spoons, and pewter mugs and turned them into bullets.

Some ladies turned their homes into hospitals when bloody soldiers stumbled in, begging for help. Because of the lack of trained doctors, these women patched up the damage caused by bullets and cannonballs. They also inoculated people against smallpox when a terrible epidemic broke out.

THANKEE, POLLY.

SHEKOLI.

Oneida Chief Shenendoah sent *Polly Cooper*, an Oneida woman, with forty warriors to deliver six hundred baskets of corn to the hungry troops at Valley Forge. She stayed behind to work as a cook for George Washington. Polly refused payment for her services, but she accepted a shawl that the officers' wives arranged to have purchased for her.

TIMELINE

1775

- British troops move to seize American ammunition and wipe out rebellion.
- Paul Revere and William Dawes ride to warn Americans of approaching British.
- The war unofficially begins as Americans fight the British in Lexington and Concord, Massachusetts.
- British declare martial law in Boston.

- American troops mobilize in New England.
- The Second Continental Congress meets in Philadelphia and establishes the Continental (American) army and navy.
- Washington named commander in chief of the Continental army.
- Battle of Bunker Hill is fought (actually fought on Breed's Hill).
- British and American troops battle each other in Canada.

- From *Phillis Wheatley*'s poem "To His Excellency, General Washington" "And so may you, whoever dares disgrace The land of freedom's heaven-defended race! Fix'd are the eyes of nations on the scales, For in their hopes Columbia's arm prevails."

· More soldiers died from diseases like smallpox, dysentery, typhoid fever, and typhus than were killed in battle. Infected troops spread disease to civilians, too.

· Exact numbers are hard to come by, but some historians believe the smallpox epidemic that swept through North America from 1775 to 1782 killed more than one hundred thousand people.

· The size of the two armies was changing constantly, but the British were always ahead. In July 1775 Washington had seventeen thousand untrained and unarmed civilians, many of them from poor backgrounds with no military experience. Washington had a hard time keeping soldiers because he couldn't pay them—sometimes he couldn't feed them either. The British already had thousands of disciplined, well-equipped soldiers in America. In 1776 they moved thirty-four thousand soldiers and sailors into New York City.

· Letter of *Hannah Winthrop*: "We were roused . . . by the beat of drum and ringing of Bell, with the dire alarm that a thousand of the Troups of George the third were gone forth to murder the peaceful inhabitants of the surrounding villages. . . ."

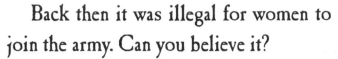

Back then it was illegal for women to join the army. Can you believe it?

But women still helped on the battlefield. Some soldiers brought their wives (and children!) with them when they enlisted. The wives cooked for the soldiers, washed their clothes, and took care of them when they were hurt. And more . . .

In the middle of battle, with bullets screaming through the air, these women carried ammunition, food, and water to the guys. If a man was hurt or killed, sometimes a woman would grab his weapon and blast away. After battles, women took care of the dead.

Margaret Corbin was the first American woman to be given a military pension. When her husband was killed in battle, Margaret loaded and fired his cannon until she was shot. Her left shoulder was destroyed, and her chest and jaw injured.

Martha Washington spent every winter at the army's winter headquarters. Martha knitted stockings for soldiers, mended clothes, cared for the sick, and arranged for her husband, George, to be as comfortable as possible.

16

· Thomas Paine publishes *Common Sense*, an instant bestseller that challenges British authority and makes the case for independence in plain language.
· British evacuate Boston.
· Declaration of Independence is adopted.
· British occupy New York City.
· Continental Congress gives the thirteen colonies permission to set up state governments.

· Most battles take place in Mid-Atlantic and New England regions.
· Washington and his troops cross the Delaware River on Christmas night and capture Trenton, New Jersey.
· Most people called the women who cooked and cleaned for soldiers "camp followers." George Washington called them the "Women of the Army."

Catharine Greene, Rebecca Biddle, Lucy Knox, and Sarah Hull were other wives who stayed with their officer husbands despite the difficult conditions of camp life. Early in the war, Catharine turned her house into a hospital to inoculate soldiers against smallpox.

17

1776 (cont.)

· Some historians think there were twenty thousand camp followers, but no one knows for sure. In some units there was one washerwoman for every ten soldiers. In others it was one woman washing clothes for one hundred men. Nobody kept track of the number of women who died on battlefields or of disease while they worked for the army.

· Camp followers had to follow military rules like the men. If they broke a rule, they could be whipped, ducked underwater, or thrown in jail.
· Molly Pitcher was not a real woman. She is a legend, a symbol of the brave women who carried water, food, and ammunition to soldiers in the middle of battle.

A few women didn't want to stay in skirts washing stinky socks and underwear. They disguised themselves as men so they could fight as "real" soldiers. They trained, marched, and risked their lives, just like the guys.

If their secret came out, officers forced them to quit. Some of the women were arrested and punished for dressing like men. But these dames made great soldiers.

Anna Marie Lane started out as a camp follower when her husband, John, enlisted. At some point, Anna Marie put on a soldier's uniform and went into combat. She received a soldier's pension from the Virginia Assembly, and she worked as a nurse after the war.

Deborah Sampson cut her hair, dressed as a man, and lived as a male soldier for eighteen months. She was wounded twice in battle——once by a saber blow to her head and later by a gunshot in the leg. Deborah was discharged when a doctor discovered she was a woman, but she received a military pension.

18

1777

· American forces win important battles in New Jersey.
· The British attack and occupy Philadelphia.
· Congress flees Philadelphia to escape the British.
· Continental Congress passes the Articles of Confederation. The states argue about ratification and officially forming the American government until 1781.

· British troops swoop down from Canada and recapture Fort Ticonderoga.
· Americans win the Battle of Saratoga, their first major victory of the war.
· Washington's army struggles through the winter camped out in Valley Forge, Pennsylvania.

Ann (Nancy) Bailey enlisted under the name of Samuel Gay in Massachusetts in 1777. She obtained the rank of corporal but then deserted the army. She was put in jail and fined for pretending to be a man and for illegally taking bounty money given to enlisting soldiers.

Sally St. Clair was a Creole girl killed in the Battle of Savannah. The authorities did not discover she was a woman disguised as a soldier until they went to bury her.

At the fierce Battle of Oriskany, **Tyonajanegen**, an Oneida woman, fought alongside her husband, Tewahongarahkon (Han Yerry Doxtator). In addition to firing her own pistols, Tyonajanegen loaded her husband's rifle for him after he was shot through the wrist. After the battle, she rode out to nearby towns to spread news of what had happened.

19

1777 (cont.)

· Dressing as a man was the biggest challenge for girls who wanted to fight. Many soldiers were young teenagers, so having a high-pitched voice and no beard was easy to explain. Soldiers slept in their uniforms and rarely bathed, so that helped. The biggest problems arose when female soldiers were injured and doctors examined them. Going to the bathroom in private was hard too.

· American soldiers faced three enemies: the British, disease, and their own stomachs. They often had to steal crops from fields or beg farmers for meals.

· In Native American societies, women had power and authority. Some fought as warriors, while others sat on important tribal councils. *Nanyehi* (also known as *Nancy Ward*) was a Cherokee warrior, leader, and diplomat. When other Cherokee leaders wanted to attack Americans, it was Nanyehi who convinced them not to.

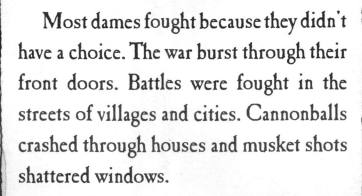

Most dames fought because they didn't have a choice. The war burst through their front doors. Battles were fought in the streets of villages and cities. Cannonballs crashed through houses and musket shots shattered windows.

British soldiers invaded American homes demanding food and supplies. Sometimes they just wanted to kill people. Desperate women picked up guns, swords, and hatchets to protect their families.

When a large group of Loyalist soldiers attacked her home in Spartenburg, South Carolina, *Jane Thomas* and her children fired their rifles so quickly the Loyalists thought the house was filled with soldiers. When the Loyalists charged the building, Jane grabbed a sword and stepped onto her front porch. Waving the sword in the air, she dared the soldiers to attack. The Loyalists retreated.

- France joins the American cause and declares war against Britain.
- British retreat from Philadelphia. Congress moves back in.
- The battleground expands to include the Western Frontier.
- Some Native Americans join with British troops to massacre settlers.
- The British are surprised by Rebel resistance in the Southern states. They again offer freedom to American slaves who join the British side. The American Congress does not offer freedom to slaves for fighting on their side, though a few state militias do.
- The only county in Georgia named for a woman is Hart County—named for *Nancy Hart.*

· The winter encampment of 1777–1778 in Valley Forge was *not* the harshest conditions endured by the men and women who worked for the American Army. Two years later, the army waited out the winter (battles were postponed until warmer months) in Morristown, New Jersey. The winter of 1779–1780 was the worst ever experienced in recorded American history until that date. The entire country suffered extremely low temperatures. Saltwater harbors froze solid for a month; rivers were choked with ice. Deep snow made travel and the delivery of supplies almost impossible. Washington's troops went days without food. Some ate bark

· Sixteen-year-old *Betsy Ambler* of Virginia understood the real impact of war. She wrote, "War in itself however distant is indeed terrible, but when brought to our very doors, when those we most love are personally engaged in it, when our friends and neighbors are exposed to its ravages . . . the reflection is overwhelming."

Pioneer dames were extra tough. They fought off enemy troops by pouring boiling water on them and firing muskets from frontier forts.

Some worked as scouts for the army, leading troops through the wilderness and preventing ambushes.

Ann Hennis Bailey wore a man's buckskin clothes and rode a black stallion named Liverpool. During the war, Ann worked as an army courier and scout in West Virginia, receiving regular army pay and rations from the patriots.

22

1779

· British and Loyalists burn towns in Connecticut and Virginia.
· Americans suffer another major defeat in Savannah, Georgia.
· Troops battle each other from Georgia to New York.
· In the late eighteenth century, the frontier extended from Lake Ontario down through the Ohio River valley and south through the Carolinas.
· "I did not feel half so frighten'd as I expected to be. Tis amazing how we get reconciled to such things. Six months ago the bare idea of being with ten, aye, twenty miles, of a battle, wou'd almost have distracted me. And now, tho' two such large armies are within six miles of us, we can converse calmly of it," wrote fifteen-year-old *Sally Wister*, outside Philadelphia.

1779 (cont.)

· Things that were affordable before the war became very expensive after the fighting began. At one point, a barrel of wheat cost more than four months of a soldier's pay.

· The money issued by the new American government was called a Continental dollar. In September 1777 a Continental dollar was worth one hundred cents. A year later, it was worth twenty-five cents. By March 1779 a dollar was worth only ten cents. This is where the expression "not worth a Continental" comes from.

The war dragged on and on. American troops were suffering big-time. They needed food, clothes, blankets, and guns, but the government was out of money. How can anyone fight when almost naked and starving?

A group of fancy Philadelphia ladies came to the rescue. They went house to house, and wrote letters asking for donations. Some people were horrified—ladies weren't supposed to do things like that!

These dames did.

It worked. Women around the country collected donations too, and they sent them to Philly. The money poured in.

Washington was so impressed he even wrote a thank-you note.

24

OOO LALA!

STEADY, GIRLS.

· The British capture Charleston, South Carolina, in America's worst defeat of the war.
· Benedict Arnold betrays America, flees to England.
· Fighting in the South becomes vicious and brutal. Soldiers from both sides are murdered after surrendering.
· Some American soldiers mutiny because they don't have enough food, clothing, and ammunition. Congress struggles to supply the army.

· In a month the Ladies Association collects 300,000 Continental dollars (about $7,500 hard currency—a huge amount of money in those days) from sixteen hundred people. The organizers want the money to go directly to the soldiers so they can buy themselves needed clothes, boots, and food. George Washington refuses. He is afraid that if his desperate men are given any cash, they will leave the army and head home to their struggling families.

Esther de Berdt Reed and thirty-six women formed the Ladies Association of Philadelphia: the first national organization of women. They began the first female fund-raising campaign, collecting money for the suffering and unpaid soldiers.

When Esther suddenly died, Sarah Franklin Bache and four other women—Anne Francis, Henrietta Hillegas, Mary Clarkson, and Susan Shippen Blair—took over.

· The Ladies Association reluctantly agrees and uses the money they raised to purchase linen cloth. The women gather, armed with needles and thread. They sew more than two thousand shirts for the soldiers, each one embroidered inside the collar with the name of the woman who stitched it.

· Martha Jefferson is too sick to go door-to-door, but she writes letters to her friends asking them to donate money to the cause.
· Some bachelors want to subscribe to the fund-raiser in the hopes that it will improve their chances of getting a date.

The American Revolution lasted for eight long years (1775–1783).

By the end of the war, thousands of soldiers and regular people were dead. Tens of thousands were hurt or disabled. Houses were robbed and burned, barns and shops destroyed, animals stolen, and crops ruined.

Our world had changed forever.

Eliza Wilkinson, a young widow in South Carolina, watched British soldiers steal her clothes and horses before destroying her home and smashing her beehives. Eliza and other women fought back by stealing British supplies and smuggling them to American troops.

26

1781

· Articles of Confederation are finally adopted. They represent the first Constitution of the United States.
· Major battles rage throughout the South, particularly in Virginia.
· French fleet drives the British Navy out of Chesapeake Bay.
· American and French troops trap the British Army at Yorktown, Virginia. The surrender of Lord Cornwallis ends the standoff.

· Some estimate that 1 percent of the population died in the Revolution—about twenty-five thousand people. If that were to happen today, that would mean nearly three million people dead.
· During the battle for New York City, so many houses burned that 25 percent of the population had no place to live. The British claimed the fire was set by a patriot woman who did not want the vital city to fall into the hands of the enemy.

In 1778 *Rachel Wells*, a widow, loaned the state of New Jersey two thousand pounds, an enormous sum of money in those times. She was robbed several times during the war, by soldiers from both armies. (Neither New Jersey nor the Continental Congress paid her back!)

27

· In her petition for financial reimbursement after the war, *Rachel Wells* wrote, "if She did not fight she threw in all her mite which bought ye Sogers [soldiers] food & Clothing & Let Them habe Blankets. . . ."
· *Hannah Ogden Caldwell*, mother of nine, was killed when invading British soldiers shot into the bedroom where she was hiding with some of her children.

· In her account of the war years, *Azubah Norton* wrote, "There was so much Suffering, and so many alarms in our neighborhood in those hard times, that it has always been painful for me to dwell upon them."

Not all of the changes were bad. With the men away at war, women had learned how to run family farms and businesses. Some became printers, weavers, carpenters, and shopkeepers. A few even became blacksmiths. Their work helped the economy stay alive.

Before the war, folks said that women and girls shouldn't think or talk about politics. The war changed that, too.

Abigail Adams took over the management of her family's farm when her husband, John, traveled for the Continental Congress. The farm thrived under Abigail's supervision.

28

OH, JOHN – YOU MISSPELLED CONTINENTAL.

NOT AGAIN!

1782
· Loyalists begin moving to Canada.
· Last battle between British and American forces is fought in South Carolina.
· Parliament votes to end the war.
· British representatives sign Articles of Peace, the preliminary peace treaty.
· British troops leave Charleston, South Carolina.

1783
· Peace treaty signed by British and Americans in Paris.
· The last British troops leave New York.
· Other nations of the world formally recognize the United States of America.
· Washington resigns his command of the army.
· Congress disbands army.
· Massachusetts declares slavery illegal.

A MOST IMPRESSIVE DECLARATION, MADAME GODDARD.

THANKEE.

When their husbands died, both *Jane Burgess* of Maryland and *Elizabeth Hager* of Boston took over their forges and became blacksmiths. Elizabeth was also a gunsmith and repaired guns and cannon for the Continental army.

Mary Katherine Goddard ran a newspaper, *The Maryland Journal*, and a printing business. The Continental Congress hired her to print the first edition of the Declaration of Independence that listed the names of all fifty-two signers.

GIVE ME THE TOOLS AND I'LL GET THE

29

1784
· Congress makes New York City the temporary capital of the United States.

1785
· Congress debates trade and commerce issues.
· Britain refuses to send an ambassador to the United States.
· *Hannah Bunce Watson* takes over the running of the *Hartford Courant* after her husband dies of smallpox.

When life went back to normal, people wrote down stories about the Revolution. Mostly they wrote about the politicians and the generals, but if you know where to look, you can find the stories of regular people, too.

Thanks to their hard work and sacrifice—women and men, girls and boys—we became a free and independent country: the United States of America.

Mercy Otis Warren wrote pamphlets, essays, plays, and poems supporting the patriotic cause. She was related to some of the Revolution's leaders and exchanged letters and ideas with many of them. Mercy also wrote an important three-volume history of the Revolution.

30

DID YOU REALLY KNOW ALL THESE REBELS?

OH YES!

COOL.

WERE PRESIDENT WASHINGTON'S TEETH MADE OUT OF WOOD?

1786

· The Virginia General Assembly declares that it is illegal to discriminate on the basis of religion. This statute influences the First Amendment of the U.S. Constitution.
· Delegates from five states meet to discuss promoting trade.

1787
· After a rebellion of farmers in New England, Congress decides to strengthen the central government.
· Constitutional Convention develops the Constitution.
· Congress decides how to govern territories west of the Ohio River with the Northwest Ordinance.
· The Young Ladies Academy of Philadelphia opens, one of the country's first schools for girls.

"We possess a Spirit that will not be conquered."

—*Abigail Adams*, in a letter to her husband, John, who became the second American president, in 1797.

"It is not in numbers, but in unity, that our great strength lies...." From *Common Sense*, by *Thomas Paine*.

32

TIMELINE

1788
· U.S. Constitution is ratified.
· The old Congress, under Articles of Confederation, adjourns.

1789
· The new government, created by the new Constitution, takes control.
· George Washington becomes first president of the United States.
· Washington proclaims a national day of Thanksgiving in November. This is not celebrated again until 1863.
· Beginning of the French Revolution.
· Girls in Boston allowed to attend public schools.

1790
· The temporary U.S. capital moves to Philadelphia, where it remains for ten years.
· The House of Representatives votes to locate the permanent capital along the banks of the Potomac River.

1791
· Bill of Rights ratified by three-fourths of the states.

> "I take leave to congratulate my fair country-women, on the
> happy revolution which the few past years has made in their favour; that in these
> infant republics, where, within my remembrance, the use of the needle was the principal
> attainment which was thought necessary for a woman, the lovely proficient is now permitted
> to appropriate a moiety of her time to studies of a more elevated and elevating nature."
>
> From *The Gleaner*, by *Judith Sargent Murray*

★ EVEN MORE DAMES ★

TEA-FREE DAMES

Penelope Pagett Barker and *Elizabeth King* held a "tea-free" party at Elizabeth's house in Edenton, North Carolina, in 1774. Fifty-one women gathered there and signed the Edenton Ladies' Agreement, promising not to buy anything British and to do everything they could to support the patriotic cause.

Sarah Fulton was the "Mother of the Boston Tea Party." She disguised her brother, husband, and other men as Mohawk Indians. These men crept aboard three ships in Boston Harbor during the night of December 16, 1773, and dumped 342 casks of tea overboard. After the attack, Sarah helped the men clean off their disguises so they wouldn't be arrested. Later, she took care of soldiers wounded in the Battle of Breed's Hill (sometimes called the Battle of Bunker Hill) and snuck messages to Washington's troops through enemy lines.

SPYING DAMES

Lydia Darragh's house was occupied when the British took over Philadelphia. British general Sir William Howe, head of the British forces, moved into the house across the street from Lydia and sometimes used her parlor for strategy meetings. Lydia eavesdropped on the British. She took notes in shorthand and folded them as small as possible. Some historians believe she sewed the notes into big buttons on the jacket of her fourteen-year-old son, John. He would slip out of the city and make his way to Washington's camp, where Lydia's older son, Lieutenant Charles Darragh, was waiting. Charles transcribed the notes and passed them to General Washington. Others point to the stories that Lydia herself delivered the news of a planned attack, while pretending to walk to a mill to buy flour. Her details of the numbers of British cannons and troops helped Washington prepare for the Battle of Whitemarsh.

Emily Geiger was twenty-one years old when she volunteered to take a message from General Thomas Sumter to General Nathanael Greene. The problem? Gen. Greene's forces were more than one hundred miles away through the swamps of South Carolina. Emily memorized the message, then folded up the paper it was written on. After two days of hard riding, Emily was captured by Tories. When their backs were turned, she ate the message. When the Tories searched her, they found nothing. When they let her go, Emily rode straight to Greene's camp and delivered the message.

Laodicea "Dicey" Langston heard reports that a cruel group of Loyalists called the "Bloody Scouts" were preparing to attack the settlement where her brothers and other militia members were hiding. The fifteen-year-old, who had been keeping track of the number of Loyalist soldiers, ran though a swamp and crossed a river at night to get word to the Americans. When Loyalists later broke into the Langston home and threatened her father, Dicey threw herself in front of him and told the soldiers to shoot her first. They didn't.

1818 · Author and poet *Elizabeth Fries Lummis Ellet* is born in Sodus Point, New York. Granddaughter of a Revolutionary War veteran, Elizabeth was the first to collect and publish stories of women's contributions to the Revolution in 1848. She was educated at a girls' school in Aurora, New York (near Seneca Falls). Ellet's early work was published in *Godey's Lady's Book*, which was edited by *Sarah Josepha Hale*, the first female magazine editor in America and the daughter of a Revolutionary War veteran.

1848 · The first Women's Rights Convention is held in Seneca Falls, New York. *Elizabeth Cady Stanton* uses the Declaration of Independence as her guide when she writes the "Declaration of Sentiments," which calls for women to be granted the same rights as men.

Grace and *Rachel Martin* were sisters-in-law who lived in South Carolina. When they heard that British soldiers carrying important messages would be passing close by their home, they knew they had to act. The two women dressed as men, grabbed their muskets, and headed out the door. They stopped the messengers at gunpoint and forced them to turn over the papers. The messages were sent to American headquarters, and the women returned home.

Anna Strong was part of the Culper ring, a group of American spies who reported on British movements in and around New York City. When information needed to be passed through British lines, she would hang her black petticoat and handkerchiefs on her clothesline to alert the other spies in the ring. Some believe that she was the lady spy referred to in the American spy code as "355."

CARING DAMES

Maria Cronkite was a washerwoman for the officers in her husband's regiment.

In the winter of 1777–1778, *Mary Frazer (Fraier)* spent her days gathering blankets and clothes from her neighbors. At night, she mended, patched, and darned what she had collected so it would be good enough to give to the soldiers at Valley Forge. She also smuggled in a plea for help from American soldiers who were starving to death in British captivity.

Sarah Osborn worked as a cook for her husband's unit. She marched with the unit from New York to Virginia. During the Battle of Yorktown, Sarah cooked and carried beef and bread to the fighting men. When George Washington asked Sarah if she was afraid of the cannonballs, she said, "It would not do for the men to fight and starve, too."

Margaret Vliet Warne was a midwife, so she knew a lot about medicine. She traveled for miles to treat injured soldiers for free.

BATTLE-HARDY DAMES

Ann Robertson Johnston Cockrill, Charlotte Robinson, and fourteen-year-old *Rachel Donelson* (future wife of Andrew Jackson, seventh president of the United States) defended forts against the British in what is now Tennessee. They poured boiling water on their attackers, set trained mastiffs on them, and fired muskets.

Elizabeth Gilmore was paid as a private by the Continental army, and was listed as a "ranger on the frontier."

Catherine Schuyler set her own wheat fields on fire so that invading British troops would not be able to use the grain.

In 1780 British forces attacked families trapped in Middle Fort, also called Middleburgh, New York. There were some militia members in the fort, but they had very little ammunition, creating a desperate situation for those trapped inside. While the cannons roared and bullets flew, *Angelica Vrooman* calmly went into action. She sat by the fire with a bullet mold, an iron spoon, and all the lead she could find. Angelica made bullets as fast as she could for the entire battle.

Sixteen-year-old *Elizabeth (Betty) Zane* saved an entire fort full of people when it was attacked by British and Native American forces. The Americans in Fort Henry quickly ran out of gunpowder. Elizabeth slipped out of the fort and sprinted sixty yards to her brother's cabin where the gunpowder was stored. She filled her apron with the gunpowder and raced back while all the enemy guns were shooting at her. With Elizabeth's gunpowder, the settlers were able to hold off the attackers until American reinforcements arrived.

⭐ FACT OR FICTION? ⭐

Many stories of Revolutionary girls and women were handed down through families. Without documents or other proof, it's hard to verify the accuracy of these stories. However, these tales give us some insight into the roles of girls and women during this crazy time. The following women and girls probably had some hand in supporting the American cause, but we will never know for sure if the details of their activities are true.

POSSIBLY TRUE, POSSIBLY FALSE

Thirteen-year-old *Phoebe Fraunces* might have helped save George Washington's life. Phoebe's father, Sam, was a famous African-American chef and restaurant owner in New York City. Phoebe helped him in the family restaurant, Fraunces Tavern, while the American army occupied New York.

One of Washington's bodyguards was actually a British spy. Some people say that Phoebe discovered this spy was trying to kill Washington by poisoning the general's peas, one of his favorite dishes. The peas were tossed into the chicken yard. The chickens ate the peas and died.

The bodyguard died too. He was convicted of treason and hanged in front of a crowd of twenty thousand people.

1865 · Slavery is abolished by the Thirteenth Amendment to the Constitution.

Patience Lovell Wright was a famous American artist who moved to London in 1772. She sculpted wax busts of the most important people in England, including King George III and Queen Charlotte. Some people think Patience learned about British plans for the war during her conversations with the royal family and leaders of Parliament. Patience wrote down the gossip she heard and hid the messages in sculptures that she shipped to her sister in America and to Benjamin Franklin in France.

Hannah Osgood was a tavern owner in New Hampshire who made bullets for the American cause. She demanded to sign the Association Test as a sign of her patriotism, even though women weren't allowed. Hannah signed and the men didn't argue.

When *Abi Humaston* had to feed a group of British soldiers, it is said that she made them a very special dish: sausage stuffed with turnip and bits of flannel cloth.

Mrs. Trefethren refused to allow British sailors to use her well to fill their ship's water casks. They ignored her and filled the casks anyway. Mrs. Trefethren waited until the sailors were busy in town; then she emptied the casks. Some say she smashed them with her axe, as well.

MOSTLY FALSE

What about *Betsy Ross*? Most historians believe that the story of Betsy sewing the first Stars and Stripes is a legend. Betsy was an upholsterer who sewed tents and uniforms for the Continental army, but her involvement with the first flag is questionable.

TOTALLY FALSE

Molly Pitcher is a mythic figure, not a real person. Most "Molly Pitcher" stories feature a woman carrying pitchers of water to thirsty men on a scorching battlefield. The water is also used to cool overheated cannons. When the man in charge of the cannon falls injured or dead, the Molly Pitcher figure takes his place. In some versions of this story, George Washington stops by to congratulate the valiant woman after the battle, sometimes giving her a small gift.

Like many myths, the Molly Pitcher story is grounded in fact. There were camp followers who helped fire cannon in desperate battles. Several textbooks identify Molly Pitcher as *Mary Ludwig Hays McCauley* of Carlisle, Pennsylvania, and claim that Mary/Molly did her famous deed at the Battle of Monmouth, New Jersey. These recountings include paintings done seventy or more years after the war as "proof" that Mary was indeed Molly.

The story of Molly Pitcher passed from folktale into "truth" in 1876, when America celebrated the centennial of the Declaration of Independence. However, there is a mountain of historical documents that prove that Mary did not do what the mythic Molly is supposed to have done. While there was a woman whose skirt was ripped by a cannonball (she was not hurt) at the Battle of Monmouth, there is nothing that proves it was Mary.

Many historians have tried to clear up the misconceptions about Molly Pitcher. See chapter 2, "Molly Pitcher," *Founding Myths: Stories That Hide Our Patriotic Past,* by Ray Raphael, (New York: New Press, 2004) for the best examination of the primary source evidence and distorted retellings of the Molly Pitcher story.

⭐ THE OTHER AMERICANS ⭐
LOYALISTS

Not everybody supported the Revolution. It is impossible to prove the numbers precisely, but many historians think that 40 percent of the American colonists wanted to be free of British rule. Another 40 percent did not choose sides and tried to stay neutral. The last 20 percent supported the British and did not want independence—they were the Loyalists. (Some people changed their minds about which side they supported. Others switched back and forth between sides, depending on who was winning.)

Loyalist women made the same kinds of sacrifices that patriot women made. Those who owned shops watched in horror when mobs smashed their merchandise. Loyalist women like *Ann Bates* acted as spies. Loyalist mothers and daughters tricked and fought American soldiers, lost their homes to their enemies, and supported the men of their families on the battlefield.

By the end of the war, the Loyalists had lost everything. Their businesses and property were taken away from them. Tens of thousands were forced to move to England or Canada, leaving everything they had ever known behind. Those who stayed in America had to start their lives from scratch and find a way to reconcile and live in peace with their neighbors.

AFRICAN AMERICANS

The phrase "life, liberty, and the pursuit of happiness" in the Declaration of Independence did not apply to African Americans. In 1776 slavery was legal in all Thirteen Colonies. One in five Americans was a slave; nearly half a million people were not free. In Virginia, the home state of George Washington, Thomas Jefferson, James Madison, and Patrick Henry, 40 percent of the population was enslaved.

The white people who made decisions about the course of the Revolution had very different ideas about what liberty should mean for African Americans.

PATRIOTS: At the beginning of the war, Washington would not allow free African Americans to enlist, though African American volunteers had sacrificed their lives at Lexington and Concord and at Bunker Hill. After Washington changed his mind, about five thousand free blacks fought for the patriot cause, and African American women worked as camp followers. Slaves worked for the patriots too, if their owners signed them up. Occasionally, an owner would free a slave who had fought and survived.

In 1778 Rhode Island offered freedom to male slaves who would fight in the state's regiment, but the slaves had to have permission from their owners to enlist. Other Northern states followed Rhode Island's lead, but women were not part of this plan.

An enslaved Massachusetts woman was the spark for that state's move to free all its slaves. In 1781 *Mumbet* found a lawyer who argued that the Massachusetts Constitution of 1780 promised liberty for all, therefore no one could be held as a slave. The court agreed and the woman was freed. She took the name of *Elizabeth Freeman*. Her case helped lay the groundwork for the abolition of slavery in Massachusetts in 1783.

BRITISH & LOYALISTS: The British promised to free any slave who ran away and joined them. This seemed like true liberty to the people held in bondage. There was one hitch: slaves owned by Loyalists who ran to the British would be returned to their owners. The British were not interested in human rights. They wanted to ruin the patriot economy, but not hurt their supporters.

Some of the escaped slaves who made it to British camps found themselves in terrible circumstances. The British turned away many escaping slaves, leaving them trapped in hostile territory with no food or resources. They sometimes forced the African Americans back into bondage, putting them to work on Loyalist plantations or selling them in the Caribbean. Others found liberation with the British. They were able to work for pay for the first time. They reunited with family members and started on their lives in freedom.

At the end of the war, almost three thousand former slaves left New York City with departing British troops, hoping to start a new life in Loyalist settlements in Canada. The settlements were a cruel disappointment. The former slaves were given the worst plots of land. Worse still, some were kidnapped and sold back into slavery.

Freedom for all Americans would not come until 1865, at the end of another long, bloody war.

NATIVE AMERICANS

At the time of the Revolutionary War, there were eighty-five Indian nations living east of the Mississippi River. Colonial Americans had been stealing their tribal lands and slaughtering them for generations.

The British promised protection and security to the Native Americans. Not surprisingly, most tribes sided with the British. The war gave them a chance to reclaim what had been taken from them and to protect their future.

Degonwadonti (also known as *Molly Brant*) was a powerful Mohawk leader married to Sir William Johnson, the British Northern Superintendent of Indian Affairs. After Johnson died in 1774, Degonwadonti and her brother, Mohawk chief Thayendanegea (Joseph Brant), fought with the British. When the British were defeated, the Crown gave Degonwadonti land in Canada in appreciation for all she had done for them during the war.

The Delaware and Shawnee sided with the patriots at the beginning of the war. When American forces attacked and killed members of their tribes, they joined with the British, too.

The Oneida, Catawba, Wappinger, and Tuscarora tribes sided with the patriots throughout the Revolution. The Treaty of Fort Stanwix of 1784 guaranteed that they would be allowed to own the land they had settled on, but the treaty was worthless. White settlers soon occupied their lands.

1920 · Women are granted the right to vote by the Nineteenth Amendment to the Constitution.
Finally!

37

> *"The history of the revolution will be one continued lie from one end to the other."*
> —John Adams, commenting bitterly about the post-Revolution adoration of George Washington and Benjamin Franklin

AUTHOR'S NOTE

This book may surprise you. It probably contains information that you didn't know before.

That's why I wrote it.

Early historians and writers did not let the facts of the American Revolution get in the way of a good story. Mason Weems (who falsely advertised himself as "Parson" Weems) lied about George Washington and the chopping down of the cherry tree. He knew Americans would buy more of his books if he filled them with uplifting, moral tales about our first president. Henry Wadsworth Longfellow made up details about Paul Revere's ride, turning the real man—who was part of a large network of patriots—into a solitary hero.

Victorian-era historians ignored or fudged the truth of many patriotic women and girls who fought for our country. Their histories reflected their world's opinion that the proper place for a woman was in the home, doing domestic chores.

The way we look at women and the way we study history have changed. (Thank goodness!) Today's historians work diligently to uncover primary-source evidence and measure it within the context of its own time period. Old biases aside, many challenges face the researcher of eighteenth-century women's lives. Few documents recount the activities of women. Even fewer documents were written by women giving their own thoughts and feelings. Last, but not least, life is confusing and disrupted in any war situation.

This book could not have been written were it not for the countless historians who have labored in archives for the past two generations. They are bringing the participation of all peoples involved in the American Revolution to light. I strongly encourage you to read through the books listed in the bibliography to learn more.

I would particularly like to thank Professor Carol Berkin, teacher of early American and women's history at the Weissman School of Arts & Sciences of Baruch College, for kindly and carefully reviewing this book. Countless librarians and teachers have encouraged me on this project for years—many thanks to them for all their encouragement.

Deepest thanks and appreciation also go to Jim Heins and Peter Golia, who reviewed this book to ensure that it accurately described the activities of the people of the Oneida Nation during the Revolution.

Thanks also to my editor, the fearless Kevin Lewis, and his delightfully organized assistants, first Joanna Feliz, then Julia Maguire, for all of their help in bringing this book to life. Copy editors Sandra Noelle Smith and Katrina Groover patiently combed through my facts and grammar. Lucy Ruth Cummins skillfully wove layers of information together until they were seamless. Special thanks to Matt Faulkner, who breathed magic into my words and turned them into art, and Lizzy Bromley for smoothing the passage between art and text.

Most of all I want to thank my husband, Scot, for supporting this independent dame through countless trips to archives and libraries and endless revisions, and to our children—Stephanie, Jessica, Meredith, and Christian—who have patiently lived with all these ladies for a long time.

ILLUSTRATOR'S NOTE

Greetings, all you Independent Dames (and Dudes)!

I grew up in a little town called Arlington, Massachusetts, just about halfway between Boston and Concord and just up the hill from the route Paul Revere and William Dawes rode down back in 1775. When I was a kid running through Menotomy Rocks Park (Arlington used to be called Menotomy back when the Indians lived there—*menotomy* means "swift running water"), we didn't play Cops and Robbers—we played Redcoats and Minutemen. Aside from Christmas, April 19 was my favorite day of the year. April 19 was a big day for us schoolkids—not just because it was the beginning of spring break but because it was Patriots' Day—a day put aside to celebrate the heroics of our Patriot forefathers. I hope that on the next Patriots' Day folks will remember to celebrate the courage and grit of our Patriot foremothers, too.

Yep, the heroines of *Independent Dames* are very near to my heart and I had a heck of a lot of fun making the illustrations for this book. As reference for the costumes, buildings, and places in the illustrations, I used books from my personal library, the public library in my town, issues of *National Geographic*, and online websites. I used my friends and memories of the people I knew back in Arlington as models for the people in the book.

To create the artwork for *Independent Dames*, I worked in a slightly different manner than I usually do. Each page is a combination of two pieces of art—one is a black-and-white line drawing and the other is a watercolor painting. After creating the drawing, I would copy it and tape it to a light table (a big box with a slab of Plexiglas over it and very bright lights inside). Then I'd tape some watercolor paper over the drawing and apply my paint. When finished, I shipped both pieces to my art director, Lucy Ruth Cummins, and she would scan them both into her computer, combining the two pieces of art to make one illustration.

It was a lot of fun to see the result. Illustrating kids' books is a cool job! I highly recommend it to anyone who likes to draw!

BIBLIOGRAPHY
(starred titles are of particular interest to adult readers)

Bakeless, John. *Turncoats, Traitors & Heroes: Espionage in the American Revolution.* New York: Da Capo Press, 1998.

Berkin, Carol. *First Generations: Women in Colonial America.* New York: Hill and Wang, 1996.

*Berkin, Carol. *Revolutionary Mothers: Women in the Struggle for America's Independence.* New York: Alfred A. Knopf, 2005.

Bohrer, Melissa Lukeman. *Glory, Passion, and Principle: The Story of Eight Remarkable Women at the Core of the American Revolution.* New York: Atria Books, 2003.

Boller, Paul F., Jr. *Presidential Wives: An Anecdotal History.* 2nd ed. New York: Oxford University Press, 1988.

Buel, Joy Day, and Richard Buel Jr. *The Way of Duty: A Woman and Her Family in Revolutionary America.* New York: W.W. Norton, 1984.

Claghorn, Charles E. *Women Patriots of the American Revolution.* Metuchen: Scarecrow Press, 1991.

Collins, Gail. *America's Women: 400 Years of Dolls, Drudges, Helpmates, and Heroines.* New York: HarperCollins, 2003.

Crane, Elaine Forman, ed. *The Diary of Elizabeth Drinker: The Life Cycle of an Eighteenth-Century Woman.* Boston: Northeastern University Press, 1994.

DePauw, Linda Grant. *Battle Cries and Lullabies: Women in War from Prehistory to Present.* Norman: University of Oklahoma Press, 1998.

*DePauw, Linda Grant. *Founding Mothers: Women in America in the Revolutionary Era.* Boston: Houghton Mifflin, 1975.

De Pauw, Linda Grant. "Women in Combat: The American Revolutionary War Experience." *Armed Forces and Society,* 7th vol., no. 2 (Winter, 1981).

Diamant, Lincoln, ed. *Revolutionary Women in the War for American Independence: A One-Volume Revised Edition of Elizabeth Ellet's 1848 Landmark Series.* Westport: Praeger Publications, 1998.

Ellis, Joseph. *His Excellency.* New York: Knopf, 2004.

Evans, Elizabeth. *Weathering the Storm: Women of the American Revolution.* St. Paul: Paragon House, 1975.

Fenn, Elizabeth A. Pox. *Americana: The Great Smallpox Epidemic of 1775–82.* New York: Farrar, Straus & Giroux, 2001.

Fischer, David Hackett. *Liberty and Freedom: A Visual History of America's Founding Ideas,* New York: Oxford University Press, 2004.

Fleming, Thomas. *Liberty!: The American Revolution.* New York: Viking, 1997.

*Gunderson, Joan R. *To Be Useful to the World: Women in Revolutionary America, 1740–1790.* New York: Twayne Publishers, 1996.

Henriques, Peter R. *Realistic Visionary: A Portrait of George Washington.* Charlottesville: University of Virginia Press, 2006.

Hibbert, Christopher. *Redcoats and Rebels: The American Revolution Through British Eyes.* New York: Norton, 1990.

Hoffman, Ronald, and Peter J. Albert eds. *Women in the Age of the American Revolution.* Charlottesville: University Press of Virginia, 1989.

James, Edward T. *Notable American Women 1607–1950: A Biographical Dictionary, Vols 1–3.* Cambridge: Belknap Press of Harvard University Press, 1971.

Kerber, Linda K. *Women of the Republic: Intellect and Ideology in Revolutionary America.* New York and London: W. W. Norton Company, 1986. Originally published 1980 by the University of North Carolina Press Chapel Hill for the Institute of Early American History and Culture.

Ketchum, Richard M. *Divided Loyalties: How the American Revolution Came to New York.* New York: Henry Holt and Company, 2002.

Martin, James Kirby. *Benedict Arnold, Revolutionary Hero: An American Warrior Reconsidered.* New York: New York University Press, 1997.

McCullough, David. *John Adams.* New York: Simon & Schuster, 2001.

Nagel, Paul C. *Adams Women: Abigail & Louisa Adams, Their Sisters and Daughters.* New York: Oxford University Press, 1987.

Nash, Gary B. *The Unknown American Revolution: The Unruly Birth of Democracy and the Struggle to Create America.* New York: Viking, 2005.

*Norton, Mary Beth. *Liberty's Daughters: The Revolutionary Experience of American Women 1750-1800.* New York: HarperCollins, 1980.

Paine, Thomas. *Common Sense,* London: Penguin Classics, 1986. Originally published 1776.

*Raphael, Ray. *Founding Myths: Stories That Hide Our Patriotic Past.* New York: New Press, 2004.

Raphael, Ray. *A People's History of the American Revolution: How Common People Shaped the Fight for Independence.* New York: New Press, 2001.

Rose, Alexander. *Washington's Spies: The Story of America's First Spy Ring.* New York: Bantam, 2006.

Schecter, Barnet. *The Battle for New York: The City at the Heart of the American Revolution.* New York: Walker, 2002.

Schlesinger, Arthur Meier. *The Colonial Merchants and the American Revolution, 1763–1776.* New York: Ungar Press, 1957.

Taylor, Dale, *The Writer's Guide to Everyday Life in Colonial America from 1607–1783.* Cincinnati: Writer's Digest Books, 1997.

Thwaites, Reuben Gold, and Louise Phelps Kellogg eds. *Frontier Defense on the Upper Ohio, 1777–1778.* Madison: Wisconsin Historical Society, 1912.

Ulrich, Laurel Thatcher. *The Age of Homespun: Objects and Stories in the Creation of an American Myth.* New York: Vintage Books, 2001.

Wertheimer, Barbara Mayer. *We Were There: The Story of Working Women in America.* New York: Pantheon Books, 1990.

Wiencek, Henry. *Imperfect God: George Washington, His Slaves, and the Creation of America.* New York: Farrar, Straus & Giroux, 2003.

Williams, Selma R. *Demeter's Daughters: The Women Who Founded America 1587–1787.* New York: Atheneum, 1976

Withey, Lynne. *Dearest Friend: A Life of Abigail Adams,* New York: Free Press, 1981.

*Young, Alfred F. *Masquerade: The Life and Times of Deborah Sampson, Continental Soldier.* New York: Alfred A. Knopf, 2004.

WEB RESOURCES

Oneida Indian Nation: www.oneidanation.net/

The George Washington Papers at the Library of Congress 1741–1799: http://lcweb2.loc.gov/ammem/gwhtml/gwhome.html

The Gilder Lehrman Institute of American History: www.gilderlehrman.org

The Minerva Center (studies women and the military): www.minervacenter.com

Women in Military Service for America Memorial: http://199.236.85.13/index.html

INDEX: OUR INDEPENDENT DAMES